Plans & Energies

Balance your budget, schedule, and spirit.

Kate O'Brien

Plans & Energies. Copyright 2022 by Kate O'Brien. All rights reserved. First published by That One Jawn, LLC in Philadelphia, PA. Printed in the United States of America. No part of this book may be reproduced or transmitted in any form or by any means, electronic or mechanical, including photocopying, recording, or by any informational storage and retrieval system, without permission in writing from the author. The included information is not intended to replace the advice of a physician or other medical professional. As a result, the author and publisher accept no responsibility for the actions or judgements of any other party.

Join our community on Instagram
@PlansNEnergies

FIRST EDITION

Created by Kate O'Brien

Designed by Didier García

Illustrations by Natalia Navarra

ISBN: 978-0-578-94245-2

There is peace in the patterns of life.

INTRODUCTION

To manage the turmoil of today,
we need to add process where possible,
account for what comes naturally,
and allow time for care.

Financial planning

Calendar, habit, and seasonal awareness

Ritual healing and spiritual exploration

All of the above show care not just for the self, but for those within your orbit and influence.

Finding (and using, because it takes effort) the proper tools is the secret to success when it comes to accomplishing goals and living a fulfilling and effective lifestyle.

Plans & Energies is a tool that gives direction and process to the varied chaos of everyday life. It allows you to balance your budget, schedule, and spirit.

Cognitive behavioral therapy practices and the cyclical processes found in nature – like the phases of the moon, the seasons, and the growth cycle of plants – are what give life to the theories and strategies presented within this guide.

STRUCTURE

FOUNDATIONS
Answer questions like:
when, how much, and how often
- Interactive templates
- Record and list based

Template-style pages allow you to interact with the content and customize the months and dates based on the timing that works best for you.

Elements
- Monthly calendar
- Monthly budget
- Quarterly budget

CYCLES
Answer complex questions like:
why, how-to, and who
- Informational and inspirational
- Active and spiritual concepts

Pages have loose structure, artistic elements, and are typically ritually focused.

Elements
- How-Tos
- Guides
- Prompts

COGNITIVE BEHAVIORAL THERAPY
Cognitive behavioral therapy (CBT) is a psychological approach to addressing destructive or reactive thought or behavior patterns.

This practice involves recognizing an area of opportunity and adjusting to address that area via coping strategies, rituals, or positive thinking.

CBT practices are built into this guide to support you in living your best, most fulfilling life.

EXAMPLE

MONTH

March

SEASONAL CONSIDERATIONS

Spring Equinox ▸ March 20
• • •
Day = Light
• • •
Balance of Light & Dark
• • •
Worm Moon ▸ March 18
• • •
→ Prepare ←

VIBE CHECK

Mood | Health | Anxiety | Energy | Socialness | Motivation | Work

GROW • HARVEST • REST • REPEAT • PLANT •
Connect the dots

MONDAY	TUESDAY	WEDNESDAY
		New Moon
	Called AAA	
[ ]	1	2
		Caiden's 9th B'day
7	8	9
		3:30 @ Fireball
14	15	16
	Vet Appt @ 2PM	
21	22	23
	Tim's Interview 5 PM	
28	29	30

EXAMPLE

THURSDAY	FRIDAY	SATURDAY	SUNDAY	HABITS & DAILY PRACTICES
3	Em → FL 4	Lunch w/ Ladies 12:30 5	6	M T W T F S S Trainer ○ ✓ ✓ ○ ○ ○ GuaSha ✓ ○ ○ ○ ○ ○ ✓ Write ✓ ○ ○ ✓ ○ ○ ○ Cardio ○ ✓ ○ ○ ○ ○ ✓ H₂O Plants ○ ○ ○ ✓ ○ ○ ○
First Q Moon 10	11	(PTO) 12	Em Home 13	M T W T F S S Trainer ○ ✓ ✓ ✓ ○ ○ ○ GuaSha ○ ○ ✓ ○ ○ ○ ✓ Write ○ ○ ✓ ✓ ○ ○ ○ Cardio ✓ ✓ ✓ ✓ ○ ○ ✓ H₂O Plants ○ ○ ○ ✓ ○ ○ ○
Flyers w/ Kyle 5:30 17	Full Moon Uncle Kent's 70th B'day 18	Wyo → Uncle Kent's Party 19	Spring Equinox Balance ☽ 20	M T W T F S S Trainer ○ ✓ ○ ✓ ○ ○ ○ GuaSha ○ ○ ✓ ○ ○ ○ ✓ Write ✓ ○ ○ ✓ ○ ✓ ○ Cardio ○ ○ ○ ✓ ○ ✓ ○ H₂O Plants ○ ○ ○ ✓ ○ ○ ○
Don's B'day 24	Last Q Moon (PTO) Drinks w/ Brett & Sharon 25	Wyo → Laser Tag for C's B'day 26	Good Times Jam 11AM 27	M T W T F S S Trainer ○ ✓ ○ ○ ✓ ○ ○ GuaSha ○ ○ ○ ○ ○ ○ ✓ Write ○ ○ ○ ✓ ✓ ○ ○ Cardio ○ ✓ ○ ✓ ○ ○ ○ H₂O Plants ○ ○ ○ ✓ ○ ○ ○
31				M T W T F S S Trainer ○ ✓ ○ ✓ ○ ○ ○ GuaSha ○ ○ ✓ ○ ○ ○ ✓ Write ✓ ○ ○ ✓ ✓ ○ ○ Cardio ✓ ✓ ○ ○ ✓ ✓ ○ H₂O Plants ○ ○ ○ ✓ ○ ○ ○

"Our power is channeled effectively when we mirror the processes of nature. Cycles of rest next to cycles of harvest lead to moments of embodiment, which turn into time spent clearing and reflecting." — Sarah Faith Gottesdiener

EXAMPLE

MONTHLY BUDGET

January

Add these totals together for the expenses total

EXPENSES

Categories	Rent	Groceries	Food Out	Shopping	Entertainment
	925.00	112.89	52.49	26.24	16.19
		51.84	6.33	10.79	19.43
		25.56	42.64	19.99	36.00
		59.16	3.23	9.49	89.99
		30.90	9.99	36.56	
		108.00	21.04	8.47	
			30.62		
			32.94		
Total	925.00	388.35	199.28	111.54	161.61

Expenses Total 3,447.60

INCOME

Source	Amount
Salary	1822.24
Freelance 1X	641.50
Bi-Monthly (PL)	180.00
Salary	1822.24
Bi-Monthly (PL)	192.50
Total	4,658.48

REFUNDS

Source	Amount
Returns	34.03
Total	34.03

EXAMPLE

TOP LINE BUDGET

Income   4,658.48
Refunds +   34.03
Incoming _____

Savings   300.00
Expenses + 3,447.60
Outgoing _____

Net Total   944.91

Add these totals to the quarterly budget page to find patterns and identify waste

Incoming
- Outgoing
Net Total

29.50	25.00	653.00			
29.50	25.00	3.00			
10.02	25.00	19.99			
9.12	25.00	5.00			
10.40	25.00	18.00			
1.06	25.00	648.00			
8.56	25.00				
16.73	25.00				
114.83	200.00	1,346.99			

NOTES

Quality > Quantity

7

EXAMPLE

QUARTERLY BUDGET   **MONTH 1**   **MONTH 2**   **MONTH 3**

		January	February	March
Income Totals		4,658.48	5,466.72	6,518.28
Refund Totals	+	34.03	9.04	6.04
Incoming		4,692.51	5,475.76	6,524.32
Savings Totals		300.00	300.00	300.00
Expenses Totals	+	3,447.60	5,803.56	4,693.22
Outgoing		3,747.60	6,103.56	4,993.22
Net Totals		944.91	-627.80	1,531.10

```
Net total is
what you have left.
1) Pay off debt
2) Save
3) Invest
```

REFLECTIONS

Any outstanding payments? Is there anywhere you can cut back? What are you saving for?

<u>Saving for a down payment</u>
↳ 20% of 300K = 60K
↳ 5% of 300K = 15K   <u>Yikes!</u>

<u>February</u> = last round of project expenses
<u>March</u> = tax return direct deposit

✳ Things to keep an eye on ✳
    Groceries very high in March
     (twice as much as prior 2 months)

Seeds

When I have fears that I may cease to be,
I call on joyful memories and set them free.

Moments that embrace like loving hugs,
and drown out noise like a voice from above.
Small spoonfuls of time that wouldn't mean much to you or to him,
they're mostly just visions of leaves in the wind.
Things like their rustle bring me back to the moments,
when the hours were calm and the stress didn't own us.

Just remember to store those seeds of hope,
for change will come and you'll wish you brought answers to cope.

MONTH

_____

SEASONAL CONSIDERATIONS

....
....
....
....
....
....
....
....
....
....
....

VIBE CHECK

	MONDAY	TUESDAY	WEDNESDAY

THINK ABOUT WHAT YOU WANT THIS MONTH •

Draw clockwise circles within this space to manifest your intentions

Add dates, moon phases, and holidays to familiarize yourself with the month ahead.

10

THURSDAY	FRIDAY	SATURDAY	SUNDAY

HABITS & DAILY PRACTICES

M T W T F S S
○○○○○○○
○○○○○○○
○○○○○○○
○○○○○○○
○○○○○○○

M T W T F S S
○○○○○○○
○○○○○○○
○○○○○○○
○○○○○○○
○○○○○○○

M T W T F S S
○○○○○○○
○○○○○○○
○○○○○○○
○○○○○○○
○○○○○○○

M T W T F S S
○○○○○○○
○○○○○○○
○○○○○○○
○○○○○○○
○○○○○○○

M T W T F S S
○○○○○○○
○○○○○○○
○○○○○○○
○○○○○○○
○○○○○○○

"Love yourself first and everything else falls into line. You really have to love yourself to get anything done in this world." – Lucille Ball

MONTHLY BUDGET

_____

```
Add these totals together
for the expenses total
```

EXPENSES

Categories					
Total					

Expenses Total _____

INCOME

Source	Amount
Total	

REFUNDS

Source	Amount
Total	

TOP LINE BUDGET

Income _____

Refunds + _____

Incoming _____

Savings _____

Expenses + _____

Outgoing _____

Net Total _____

Add these totals to the quarterly budget page to find patterns and identify waste

```
  Incoming
- Outgoing
  Net Total
```

NOTES

"You can't connect the dots looking forward; you can only connect them looking backward." - Steve Jobs

RITUAL BATH

1 Start to think about your intentions for this experience. Focus on intangibles like creativity, healing, love, and strength.

2 Collect your crystals. Crystals can be selected to support your chosen intentions or you. Make sure to place a clear quartz near the head of the bath to help keep you balanced and focused.

3 Gather your candles, oils, salts, florals, herbs, objects, incense, and a paper and pen. Don't forget to wash items from your garden before use.

Florals and Herbs
- **DANDELIONS** heal and inspire happiness
- **PINE NEEDLES** encourage resilience
- **SAGE** cleanses and generates clarity
- **ROSES** appeal to and honor the heart
- **LAVENDER** promotes calm
- **CLOVER** brings luck and wards off evil
- **SALT** protects and balances

Objects
- **ORBS** pay homage to the sun and the moon
- **PINE CONES** symbolize regeneration
- **SHELLS** represent the moon's power
- **EGGS** stand for fertility
- **CUPS** encapsulate the chalice or the feminine
- **KEYS** embody freedom
- **SKULLS** allude to spirit

4 Add sound – doesn't matter if it's a bathroom fan or a centering playlist. Sound will help focus your energy.

Scan to listen to our Ritual Bath playlist

5 Take a deep breath.

6 Start your bath water as you begin to think about what you would like to dedicate this energy to.

7 Place the items you've gathered in and around the bath. Think about why you chose them and what they represent. Get lost in the process and let your mind wander as you intentionally place and pour each talisman.

8 Enter the new world you created for yourself. Acknowledge that you're caring for yourself physically and mentally. You're healing, seeing, and growing. As your skin welcomes the moisture of the water, open yourself up to the energies of your chosen intentions. Continue exploring your thoughts and feelings.

---

9 Acknowledge your purpose by writing it on one of the tear cards and dropping it into the water. Let the water absorb the intentions as you do.

Use the included tear cards!

10 When you're ready, ease yourself back to your environment as the water drains from the bath.

Tip — Don't put petals or paper down the drain!

Timing — Any day of the week, any time of day. Both a new and full moon offer heightened benefits.

Learn more about why on page 82.

MONTH

_____

SEASONAL CONSIDERATIONS

....
....
....
....
....
....
....
....
....
....

VIBE CHECK

PLANT · GROW · HARVEST · REST · REPEAT

Connect the dots

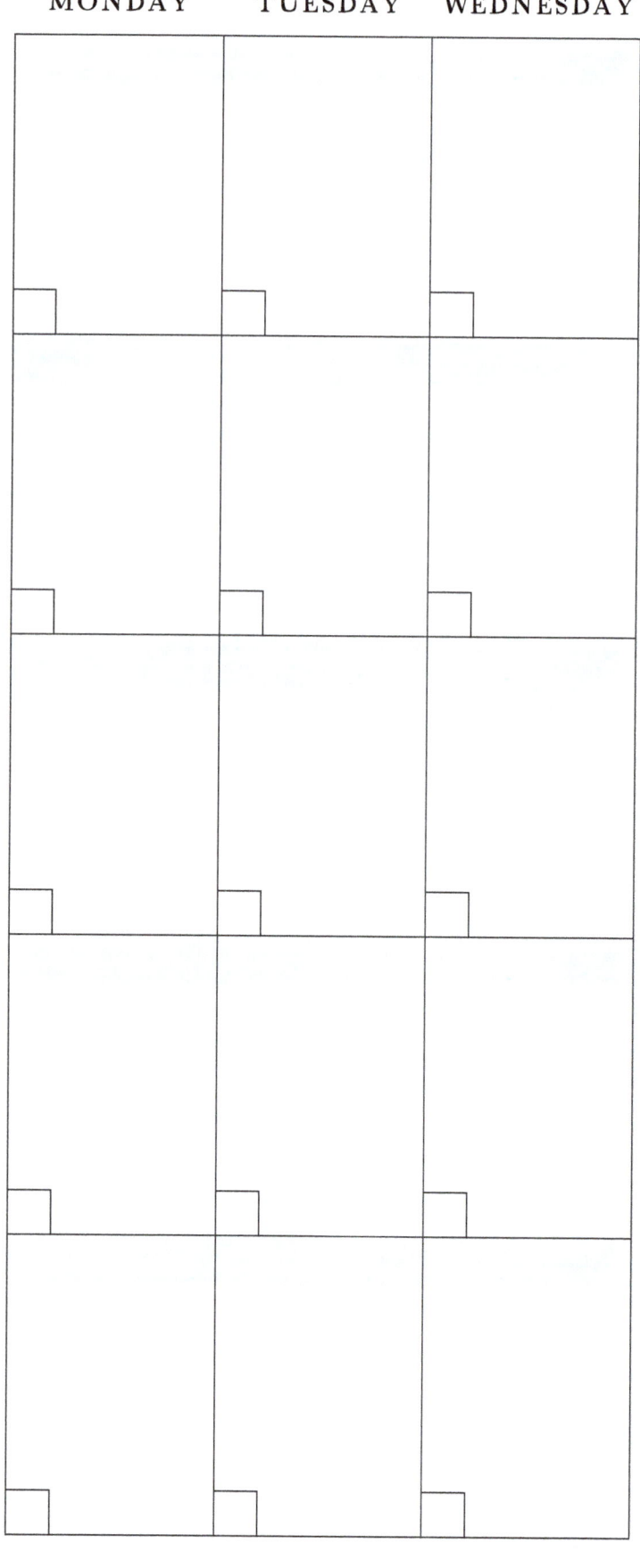

MONDAY	TUESDAY	WEDNESDAY

THURSDAY	FRIDAY	SATURDAY	SUNDAY

HABITS & DAILY PRACTICES

M T W T F S S
○○○○○○○
○○○○○○○
○○○○○○○
○○○○○○○
○○○○○○○

M T W T F S S
○○○○○○○
○○○○○○○
○○○○○○○
○○○○○○○
○○○○○○○

M T W T F S S
○○○○○○○
○○○○○○○
○○○○○○○
○○○○○○○
○○○○○○○

M T W T F S S
○○○○○○○
○○○○○○○
○○○○○○○
○○○○○○○
○○○○○○○

M T W T F S S
○○○○○○○
○○○○○○○
○○○○○○○
○○○○○○○
○○○○○○○

"Our power is channeled effectively when we mirror the processes of nature. Cycles of rest next to cycles of harvest lead to moments of embodiment, which turn into time spent clearing and reflecting." — Sarah Faith Gottesdiener

MONTHLY BUDGET

_____

Add these totals together for the expenses total

EXPENSES

Categories					
Total					

Expenses Total _____

INCOME

Source	Amount
Total	

REFUNDS

Source	Amount
Total	

TOP LINE BUDGET

Income _____

Refunds + _____

Incoming _____

Savings _____

Expenses + _____

Outgoing _____

Net Total _____

```
  Incoming
- Outgoing
  Net Total
```

Add these totals to the quarterly budget page to find patterns and identify waste

NOTES

"The most difficult thing is the decision to act, the rest is merely tenacity." - Amelia Earhart

SMUDGING RITUALS

The burning of herbs to purify has been part of spiritual practice for thousands of years.

Smudging allows you to alter the energy of a space, person, or thing with strong, earthy aromas. By changing the energy, you're able to cleanse and focus on the now without hindrance.

Getting started

Focus on your intention for this cleanse and keep that energy with you throughout the process.

Gather your incense, sage, or herbs, as well as a lighter or match. You might also need a flame-safe bowl, cauldron, or fire-safe tray for your herbs if they aren't securely gathered.

Take a moment to calm and center yourself.

Always open windows or doors if you plan to smudge inside so the energy you're looking to expel can exit the space.

Light the end of your incense or herb and blow out the flame so the end is glowing red.

What to use
SAGE
INCENSE
ROSE
LAVENDER
SWEETGRASS

What to smudge
NEW LIVING SPACE
ROOM OR ENVIRONMENT
PERSON OR BEING
OBJECTS

To smudge a space

Walk the outer edges of your space. Pay special attention to areas of focus. Watch the smoke drift behind you and slowly expand to fill the interior of the room. Smudge the outline of doors and interior spaces like closets and alcoves.

As you go about purifying the space, remember to think about the energy you want to shift. Either meditate on those intentions or say them outloud.

To smudge a being

Wrap the smoke around the head in circular motions. Go down the front of the body and take the smoke around to the back. Lift the feet and complete the ritual by allowing the smoke to drift below each foot.

It's important to follow your intuition when it comes to cleansing a being. Address areas of focus and move on when it feels right. Recall your intended outcomes as you move throughout the ritual.

 **Tips** — Never leave burning materials unattended and practice in a well-ventilated area. Leave windows and doors open beyond the active smudging ritual until all smoke has left the space.

MONTH

_____

SEASONAL CONSIDERATIONS

....
....
....
....
....
....
....
....

VIBE CHECK

MONDAY	TUESDAY	WEDNESDAY

THINK ABOUT WHAT YOU WANT THIS MONTH •
Draw clockwise circles within this space to manifest your intentions

Add dates, moon phases, and holidays to familiarize yourself with the month ahead.

| THURSDAY | FRIDAY | SATURDAY | SUNDAY |

HABITS & DAILY PRACTICES

M T W T F S S
○○○○○○○
○○○○○○○
○○○○○○○
○○○○○○○
○○○○○○○

M T W T F S S
○○○○○○○
○○○○○○○
○○○○○○○
○○○○○○○
○○○○○○○

M T W T F S S
○○○○○○○
○○○○○○○
○○○○○○○
○○○○○○○
○○○○○○○

M T W T F S S
○○○○○○○
○○○○○○○
○○○○○○○
○○○○○○○
○○○○○○○

M T W T F S S
○○○○○○○
○○○○○○○
○○○○○○○
○○○○○○○
○○○○○○○

"Change will not come if we wait for some other person or some other time. We are the ones we've been waiting for. We are the change that we seek." – Barack Obama

MONTHLY BUDGET

_____

Add these totals together
for the expenses total

EXPENSES

Categories					
Total					

Expenses Total _____

INCOME

Source	Amount
Total	

REFUNDS

Source	Amount
Total	

TOP LINE BUDGET

Income _____   Add these totals to
Refunds + _____   the quarterly budget
Incoming _____ page to find patterns
Savings _____   and identify waste
Expenses + _____

    Incoming   **Outgoing** _____
− Outgoing
    Net Total   **Net Total** _____

NOTES

"Beware of little expenses; a small leak will sink a great ship." - Benjamin Franklin

QUARTERLY BUDGET

	MONTH 1	MONTH 2	MONTH 3
Income Totals			
Refund Totals +			
Incoming			
Savings Totals			
Expenses Totals +			
Outgoing			
Net Totals			

```
Net total is
what you have left.
1) Pay off debt
2) Save
3) Invest
```

REFLECTIONS

Any outstanding payments? Is there anywhere you can cut back? What are you saving for?

Where is your magic place?

Where do you do your big thinking?
Where do you feel peaceful and safe?
Draw or describe it.

Remember this place the next time you feel uninspired, overwhelmed, or challenged.

MONTH

_____

SEASONAL CONSIDERATIONS

....
....
....
....
....
....
....
....
....

VIBE CHECK

PLANT · GROW · HARVEST · REST · REPEAT

Connect the dots

MONDAY	TUESDAY	WEDNESDAY

THURSDAY	FRIDAY	SATURDAY	SUNDAY

HABITS & DAILY PRACTICES

M T W T F S S
○○○○○○○
○○○○○○○
○○○○○○○
○○○○○○○
○○○○○○○

M T W T F S S
○○○○○○○
○○○○○○○
○○○○○○○
○○○○○○○
○○○○○○○

M T W T F S S
○○○○○○○
○○○○○○○
○○○○○○○
○○○○○○○
○○○○○○○

M T W T F S S
○○○○○○○
○○○○○○○
○○○○○○○
○○○○○○○
○○○○○○○

M T W T F S S
○○○○○○○
○○○○○○○
○○○○○○○
○○○○○○○
○○○○○○○

"Your intentions are seeds you plant in your consciousness and subconsciousness. You nourish the seeds with your actions and your energy." — Sarah Faith Gottesdiener

MONTHLY BUDGET

_____

Add these totals together
for the expenses total

EXPENSES

Categories					
Total					

Expenses Total _____

INCOME

Source	Amount
Total	

REFUNDS

Source	Amount
Total	

TOP LINE BUDGET

Income _____

Refunds + _____

Incoming _____

Savings _____

Expenses + _____

```
        Incoming
      - Outgoing
        Net Total
```

Outgoing _____

Net Total _____

Add these totals to the quarterly budget page to find patterns and identify waste

NOTES

"When prosperity comes, do not use all of it." - Confucius

FINDING CALM

Anxiety, panic, overload...

Arming yourself with tools to manage overwhelming feelings helps you stay in control during stressful situations.

These tactics work to bring your mind back to the present moment.

Use these tips when you can't see the calm through the storm.

SAY WHAT IT IS
Acknowledgment will always cause a shift in power. Speak – out loud – what you're experiencing within to expel the negativity.

5, 4, 3, 2, 1 AND DONE
Identify 5 things you can see, 4 things you can touch, 3 you can hear, 2 you can smell, and 1 you can taste. Allow your racing thoughts to slow down and recenter.

CONSCIOUS BREATHING
Seems obvious, but sometimes we need a reminder. Breathe in deeply through your nose for 7 seconds and out through your mouth for 7 seconds. Repeat as needed.

MOVE
Adjust your body or change your space to put your attention on actions, not thoughts.

If you get to a place where you're having more frequent attacks or the episodes are starting to get to be too much to manage, seek help and support from a medical professional or therapist.

Learn more about where to seek mental health support by calling 1-800-622-HELP (4357) or visiting SAMHSA.gov for information from the Substance Abuse and Mental Health Services Administration.

MONTH

SEASONAL CONSIDERATIONS

....
....
....
....
....
....
....
....

VIBE CHECK

THINK ABOUT WHAT YOU WANT THIS MONTH •

Draw clockwise circles within this space to manifest your intentions

MONDAY	TUESDAY	WEDNESDAY

Add dates, moon phases, and holidays to familiarize yourself with the month ahead.

THURSDAY	FRIDAY	SATURDAY	SUNDAY

HABITS & DAILY PRACTICES

M T W T F S S
.... ○○○○○○○
.... ○○○○○○○
.... ○○○○○○○
.... ○○○○○○○
.... ○○○○○○○

M T W T F S S
.... ○○○○○○○
.... ○○○○○○○
.... ○○○○○○○
.... ○○○○○○○
.... ○○○○○○○

M T W T F S S
.... ○○○○○○○
.... ○○○○○○○
.... ○○○○○○○
.... ○○○○○○○
.... ○○○○○○○

M T W T F S S
.... ○○○○○○○
.... ○○○○○○○
.... ○○○○○○○
.... ○○○○○○○
.... ○○○○○○○

M T W T F S S
.... ○○○○○○○
.... ○○○○○○○
.... ○○○○○○○
.... ○○○○○○○
.... ○○○○○○○

"What we fear doing most is usually what we most need to do." - Ralph Waldo Emerson

MONTHLY BUDGET

_____

Add these totals together
for the expenses total

EXPENSES

Categories					
Total					

Expenses Total _____

INCOME

Source	Amount
Total	

REFUNDS

Source	Amount
Total	

TOP LINE BUDGET

Income _____
Refunds + _____
Incoming _____
Savings _____
Expenses + _____
Outgoing _____
Net Total _____

Add these totals to
the quarterly budget
page to find patterns
and identify waste

```
  Incoming
- Outgoing
  Net Total
```

NOTES

Quality > Quantity

BURNING RITUALS

Fire rituals allow you to cleanse and release thoughts that no longer serve you. Largely associated with passion, love, and obsession, these small acts of ceremony add exclamations to your intentions for growth. Flame work should always be approached with a calm mind and clear heart.

Light a candle to complete or release a thought. Watch the flame as you think about what you want to release. Blow out the candle with control to complete the ritual. (Optional) Place the lit candle on the ground and walk over it before extinguishing. Pass between two lit candles to strengthen thoughts of transition.

Assemble a bonfire to make a powerful statement of freedom and liberate yourself from unwanted energy. Gaze upon the structure that you've built and light the bon-fire. Acknowledge your role in the process. How you focused energy to gather what was no longer needed in order to cleanse.

Light paper with a match once you've written down unwelcome feelings or unfavorable behaviors. Watch as they burn and dissolve before your eyes. Allow yourself to let them go.

Use the included tear cards!

Always consider fire safety.
Practice in a safe environment
with appropriate materials.

SELF CHECK-IN TAROT SPREAD

Use blank space for notes.

① What do I think is happening
② What is actually happening
③ What actions should I take
④ What should I keep in mind moving forward

MONTH

_____

SEASONAL CONSIDERATIONS

....
....
....
....
....
....
....
....
....

VIBE CHECK

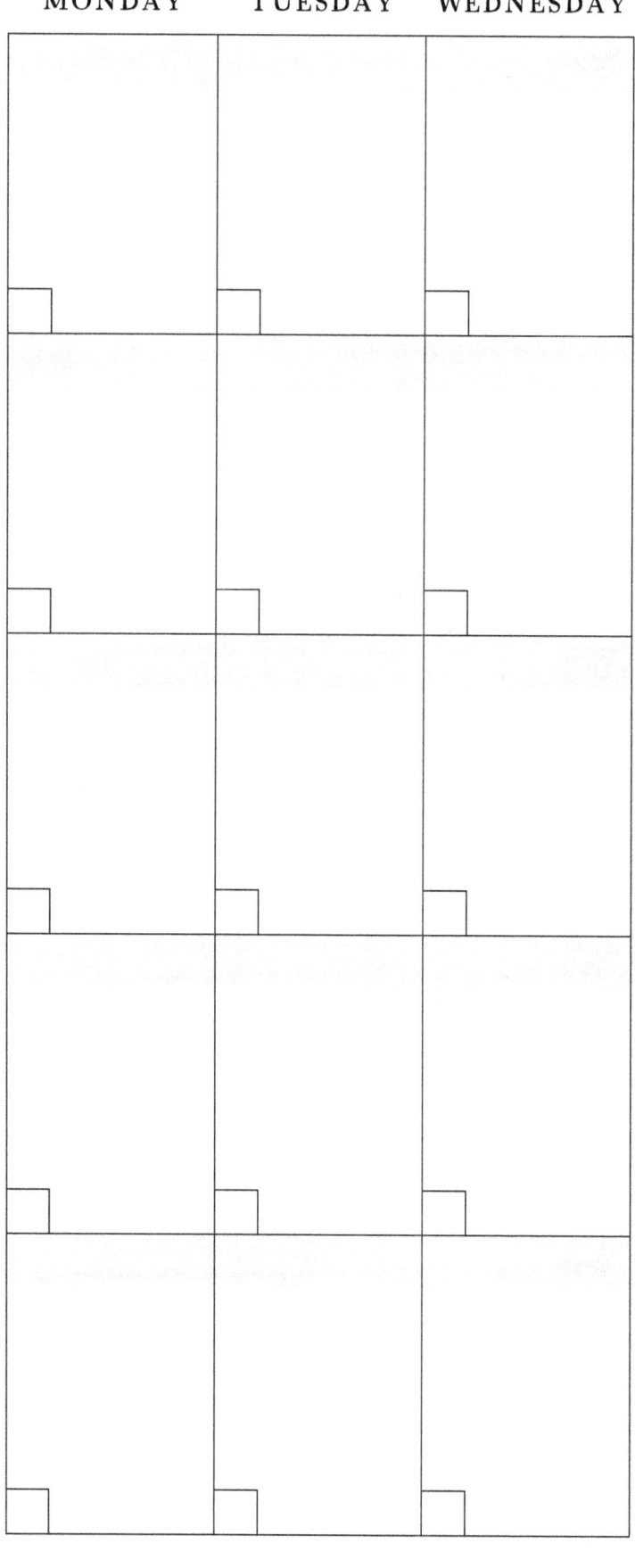

Connect the dots

PLANT · GROW · HARVEST · REST · REPEAT ·

| THURSDAY | FRIDAY | SATURDAY | SUNDAY |

HABITS & DAILY PRACTICES

M T W T F S S
○○○○○○○
○○○○○○○
○○○○○○○
○○○○○○○
○○○○○○○

M T W T F S S
○○○○○○○
○○○○○○○
○○○○○○○
○○○○○○○
○○○○○○○

M T W T F S S
○○○○○○○
○○○○○○○
○○○○○○○
○○○○○○○
○○○○○○○

M T W T F S S
○○○○○○○
○○○○○○○
○○○○○○○
○○○○○○○
○○○○○○○

M T W T F S S
○○○○○○○
○○○○○○○
○○○○○○○
○○○○○○○
○○○○○○○

"Immediate lessons that we can take from herbs are to put down roots, turn towards the light, create what we need to survive, and give back to those around us." – Judy Ann Nock

MONTHLY BUDGET

_____

```
Add these totals together
for the expenses total
```

EXPENSES

Categories					
Total					

Expenses Total _____

INCOME

Source	Amount
Total	

REFUNDS

Source	Amount
Total	

TOP LINE BUDGET

Income _____
Refunds + _____
Incoming _____
Savings _____
Expenses + _____
Outgoing _____
Net Total _____

Add these totals to the quarterly budget page to find patterns and identify waste

```
  Incoming
- Outgoing
  Net Total
```

NOTES

"Wealth is the ability to fully experience life." – Henry David Thoreau

QUARTERLY BUDGET   MONTH 1   MONTH 2   MONTH 3

	Income Totals			
	Refund Totals	+		
	Incoming			
	Savings Totals			
	Expenses Totals	+		
	Outgoing			
	Net Totals			

```
Net total is
what you have left.
1) Pay off debt
2) Save
3) Invest
```

REFLECTIONS

Any outstanding payments? Is there anywhere you can cut back? What are you saving for?

What do you think you are doing well?
Can't think of anything? Jot down some things you want to do well.

Keep adding to this list.

MONTH

_____

SEASONAL CONSIDERATIONS

....
....
....
....
....
....
....
....
....

VIBE CHECK

MONDAY	TUESDAY	WEDNESDAY

Add dates, moon phases, and holidays to familiarize yourself with the month ahead.

THINK ABOUT WHAT YOU WANT THIS MONTH

Draw clockwise circles within this space to manifest your intentions

THURSDAY　　FRIDAY　　SATURDAY　　SUNDAY

HABITS & DAILY PRACTICES

M T W T F S S

M T W T F S S

M T W T F S S

M T W T F S S

M T W T F S S

"Be patient with yourself. Self-growth is tender; it's holy ground. There's no greater investment." - Stephen Covey

MONTHLY BUDGET

_____

Add these totals together
for the expenses total

EXPENSES

Categories					
Total					

Expenses Total _____

INCOME

Source	Amount
Total	

REFUNDS

Source	Amount
Total	

TOP LINE BUDGET

Income _____

Refunds + _____

Incoming _____

Savings _____

Expenses + _____

Outgoing _____

Net Total _____

Add these totals to the quarterly budget page to find patterns and identify waste

```
    Incoming
  - Outgoing
    Net Total
```

NOTES

"Happiness is not in the mere possession of money; it lies in the joy of achievement, in the thrill of creative effort." - Franklin D. Roosevelt

MONTHLY TAROT SPREAD

Use blank space for notes.

1. Current self
2. Inspiration
3. Main theme
4. Area of growth
5. Action

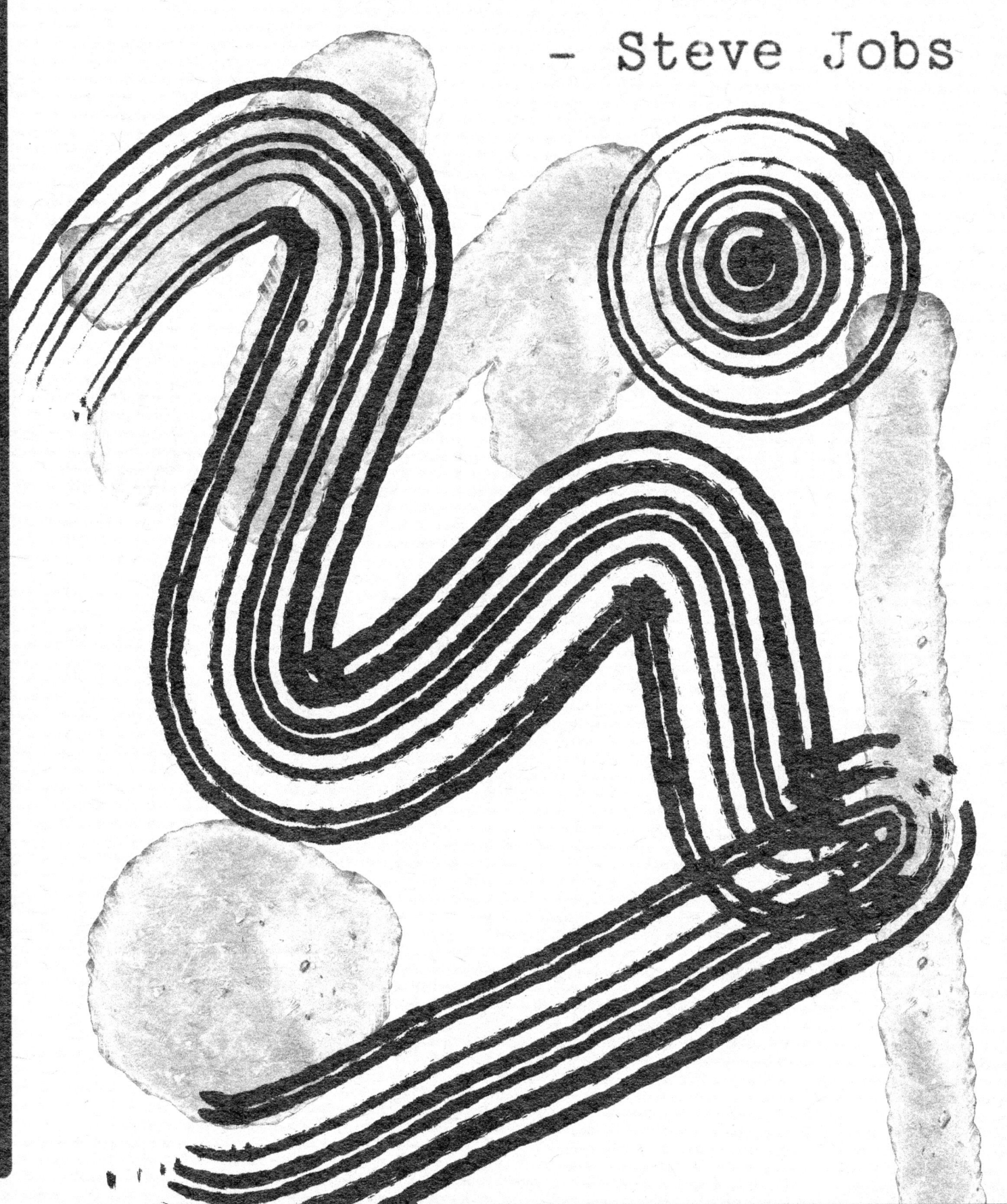

"Stay hungry.
Stay foolish."
- Steve Jobs

MONTH

_____

SEASONAL CONSIDERATIONS

....
....
....
....
....
....
....
....

VIBE CHECK

	MONDAY	TUESDAY	WEDNESDAY

PLANT · GROW · HARVEST · REST · REPEAT

Connect the dots

THURSDAY	FRIDAY	SATURDAY	SUNDAY

HABITS & DAILY PRACTICES

M T W T F S S
○○○○○○○
○○○○○○○
○○○○○○○
○○○○○○○
○○○○○○○

M T W T F S S
○○○○○○○
○○○○○○○
○○○○○○○
○○○○○○○
○○○○○○○

M T W T F S S
○○○○○○○
○○○○○○○
○○○○○○○
○○○○○○○
○○○○○○○

M T W T F S S
○○○○○○○
○○○○○○○
○○○○○○○
○○○○○○○
○○○○○○○

M T W T F S S
○○○○○○○
○○○○○○○
○○○○○○○
○○○○○○○
○○○○○○○

You are the universe. You are the world.

MONTHLY BUDGET

_____

Add these totals together for the expenses total

EXPENSES

Categories					
Total					

Expenses Total _____

INCOME

Source	Amount
Total	

REFUNDS

Source	Amount
Total	

TOP LINE BUDGET

Income _____
Refunds + _____
Incoming _____
Savings _____
Expenses + _____
Outgoing _____
Net Total _____

```
  Incoming
- Outgoing
  Net Total
```

Add these totals to the quarterly budget page to find patterns and identify waste

NOTES

"An investment in knowledge pays the best interest." – Benjamin Franklin

BIRTHDAY TAROT SPREAD

HAPPY BIRTHDAY!

Each card represents a month in your year to come.

- **1** January
- **2** February
- **3** March
- **4** April
- **5** May
- **6** June
- **7** July
- **8** August
- **9** September
- **10** October
- **11** November
- **12** December

Use blank space for notes.

MONTH

_____

SEASONAL CONSIDERATIONS

....
....
....
....
....
....
....
....

VIBE CHECK

MONDAY	TUESDAY	WEDNESDAY

THINK ABOUT WHAT YOU WANT THIS MONTH ·

Draw clockwise circles within this space to manifest your intentions

Add dates, moon phases, and holidays to familiarize yourself with the month ahead.

THURSDAY	FRIDAY	SATURDAY	SUNDAY

HABITS & DAILY PRACTICES

M T W T F S S
.... ○○○○○○○
.... ○○○○○○○
.... ○○○○○○○
.... ○○○○○○○
.... ○○○○○○○

M T W T F S S
.... ○○○○○○○
.... ○○○○○○○
.... ○○○○○○○
.... ○○○○○○○
.... ○○○○○○○

M T W T F S S
.... ○○○○○○○
.... ○○○○○○○
.... ○○○○○○○
.... ○○○○○○○
.... ○○○○○○○

M T W T F S S
.... ○○○○○○○
.... ○○○○○○○
.... ○○○○○○○
.... ○○○○○○○
.... ○○○○○○○

M T W T F S S
.... ○○○○○○○
.... ○○○○○○○
.... ○○○○○○○
.... ○○○○○○○
.... ○○○○○○○

"If everything was perfect, you would never learn, and you would never grow." – Beyoncé Knowles-Carter

MONTHLY BUDGET

_____

Add these totals together
for the expenses total

EXPENSES

Categories					
Total					

Expenses Total _____

INCOME

Source	Amount
Total	

REFUNDS

Source	Amount
Total	

TOP LINE BUDGET

Income _____
Refunds + _____
Incoming _____
Savings _____
Expenses + _____
Outgoing _____
Net Total _____

Add these totals to the quarterly budget page to find patterns and identify waste

```
  Incoming
- Outgoing
  Net Total
```

NOTES

"A goal without a plan is just a wish." - Antoine de Saint-Exupéry

QUARTERLY BUDGET | | MONTH 1 | MONTH 2 | MONTH 3 |
|---|---|---|---|
| Income Totals | | | |
| Refund Totals + | | | |
| **Incoming** | | | |
| Savings Totals | | | |
| Expenses Totals + | | | |
| **Outgoing** | | | |
| **Net Totals** | | | |

```
Net total is
what you have left.
1) Pay off debt
2) Save
3) Invest
```

REFLECTIONS

Any outstanding payments? Is there anywhere you can cut back? What are you saving for?

What aspects of life are you looking to focus on right now?

Use this space for long-term lists and priorities.

Keep adding to this list.

HOUSEPLANTS TO KNOW AND LOVE

Plants make your house feel like a home and watching them change and develop brings immeasurable joy.

These ride-or-die houseplants purify your air, act as a reminder of the cycles of life, and care for you as you care for them.

MONSTERA

Why they're great
- They're big!
- New growth is a joy to watch unravel.
- Air roots are accessible and interesting.

Things to know
- Leaves NEED to be dusted — it's the right thing to do.
- Love lots of light — but not full direct.
- Prefer filtered water. Leave sink water in a jar overnight before each 1-2 week watering.

POTHOS

Why they're great
- Grow quickly and are easy to share and propagate.
- Work well in low light but thrive in lots of it.

Things to know
- Prune dead to encourage new growth.
- Vine-like strands love to hang.
- Leaves get wilted when thirsty.

SNAKE PLANT

Why they're great
- Basically indestructible.
- Purify toxins in the air.
- Tall stems make them great for decorating.

Things to know
- Don't water often.
- Like, don't water for weeks.
- Basically forget about them and they'll thrive.

Pet friendly

PILEA

Why they're great
- Circular leaves just look happy.
- Can adapt to low light.
- Grow fast.

Things to know
- Love to be rotated.
- Propagates on its own. Separate babies into new pots to keep the family going.

`Pet friendly`

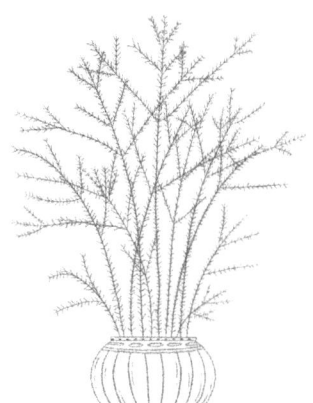

ASPARAGUS FERN

Why they're great
- Leaves look like little plant clouds.
- Love light but can manage in low light situations.
- Grow quickly.

Things to know
- Drop thin, dry leaves.
- When getting a new stalk, leaves look like little flower buds, which can resemble pests. Just give them time to pop.

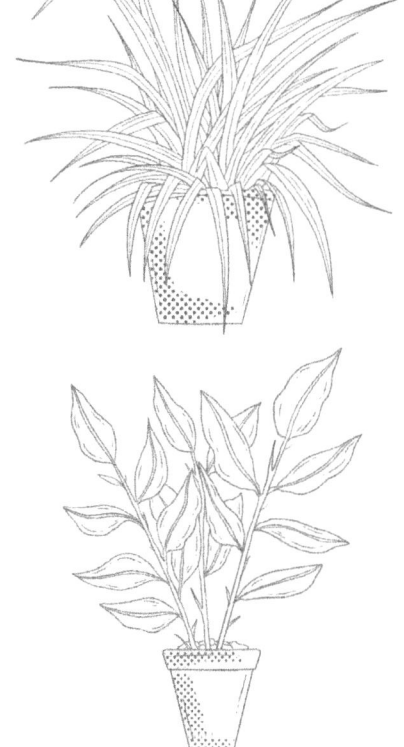

SPIDER PLANT

Why they're great
- Thrive in almost all light situations.
- Easy to propagate. Make sure babies have proper roots growing before replanting.

Things to know
- Prune dead to encourage new growth.
- Brown leaves mean you're overwatering.
- Long leaves are great for giving sculptures and other treasures great peekaboo moments.

`Pet friendly`

RUBBER PLANT

Why they're great
- Have large, smooth leaves that make you want to shake their leaf-hand.
- Can get huge if you let them.

Things to know
- Like to be restricted so keep their pots small.
- If they start to get leggy, they want more sun but not direct light.
- Leaves love to be cleaned and misted.

Tips

Place a layer of cork under your plants. It absorbs excess water. Bonus! Fungus gnats hate the smell of wet cork.

Dust leaves by placing your hand under the leaf and wiping towards you with a damp cloth.

Crystals, sticks, figurines and shells love to live in plants. Bonus! Angled sticks are great for support.

MONTH

SEASONAL CONSIDERATIONS

....
....
....
....
....
....
....
....
....
....

VIBE CHECK

PLANT · GROW · HARVEST · REST · REPEAT

Connect the dots

MONDAY	TUESDAY	WEDNESDAY

THURSDAY	FRIDAY	SATURDAY	SUNDAY	**HABITS & DAILY PRACTICES**
				M T W T F S S .... ○○○○○○○ .... ○○○○○○○ .... ○○○○○○○ .... ○○○○○○○ .... ○○○○○○○
				M T W T F S S .... ○○○○○○○ .... ○○○○○○○ .... ○○○○○○○ .... ○○○○○○○ .... ○○○○○○○
				M T W T F S S .... ○○○○○○○ .... ○○○○○○○ .... ○○○○○○○ .... ○○○○○○○ .... ○○○○○○○
				M T W T F S S .... ○○○○○○○ .... ○○○○○○○ .... ○○○○○○○ .... ○○○○○○○ .... ○○○○○○○
				M T W T F S S .... ○○○○○○○ .... ○○○○○○○ .... ○○○○○○○ .... ○○○○○○○ .... ○○○○○○○

"Sow a thought, reap an action; sow an action, reap a habit; sow a habit, reap a character; sow a character, reap a destiny." - Stephen Covey

MONTHLY BUDGET

_____

Add these totals together for the expenses total

EXPENSES

Categories					
Total					

Expenses Total _____

INCOME

Source	Amount
Total	

REFUNDS

Source	Amount
Total	

TOP LINE BUDGET

Income _____

Refunds + _____

Incoming _____

Savings _____

Expenses + _____

Outgoing _____

Net Total _____

```
  Incoming
- Outgoing
  Net Total
```

Add these totals to the quarterly budget page to find patterns and identify waste

NOTES

"With self-discipline most anything is possible." - Theodore Roosevelt

MONTH

_____

SEASONAL CONSIDERATIONS

....
....
....
....
....
....
....
....
....
....

VIBE CHECK

MONDAY	TUESDAY	WEDNESDAY

THINK ABOUT WHAT YOU WANT THIS MONTH

Draw clockwise circles within this space to manifest your intentions

Add dates, moon phases, and holidays to familiarize yourself with the month ahead.

THURSDAY	FRIDAY	SATURDAY	SUNDAY

HABITS & DAILY PRACTICES

M T W T F S S
.... ○○○○○○○
.... ○○○○○○○
.... ○○○○○○○
.... ○○○○○○○
.... ○○○○○○○

M T W T F S S
.... ○○○○○○○
.... ○○○○○○○
.... ○○○○○○○
.... ○○○○○○○
.... ○○○○○○○

M T W T F S S
.... ○○○○○○○
.... ○○○○○○○
.... ○○○○○○○
.... ○○○○○○○
.... ○○○○○○○

M T W T F S S
.... ○○○○○○○
.... ○○○○○○○
.... ○○○○○○○
.... ○○○○○○○
.... ○○○○○○○

M T W T F S S
.... ○○○○○○○
.... ○○○○○○○
.... ○○○○○○○
.... ○○○○○○○
.... ○○○○○○○

"Who looks outside, dreams; who looks inside, awakes." – Carl Jung

MONTHLY BUDGET

_____

Add these totals together
for the expenses total

EXPENSES

Categories					
Total					

Expenses Total _____

INCOME

Source	Amount
Total	

REFUNDS

Source	Amount
Total	

TOP LINE BUDGET

Income _____

Refunds + _____

Incoming _____

Savings _____

Expenses + _____

Outgoing _____

Net Total _____

Add these totals to the quarterly budget page to find patterns and identify waste

```
  Incoming
- Outgoing
  Net Total
```

NOTES

"If you don't take the time to think about and analyze your life, you'll never realize all the dots that are all connected." – Beyoncé Knowles-Carter

SEASONAL CONSIDERATIONS

There is peace in the patterns of life and the understanding that
all beings are connected in their cycles of existence. These seasonal
consistencies outline phases of growth to encourage thoughtful experience.

```
Use these themes — most often found in nature — to assist
you in navigating the ebb and flow of everyday life.
```

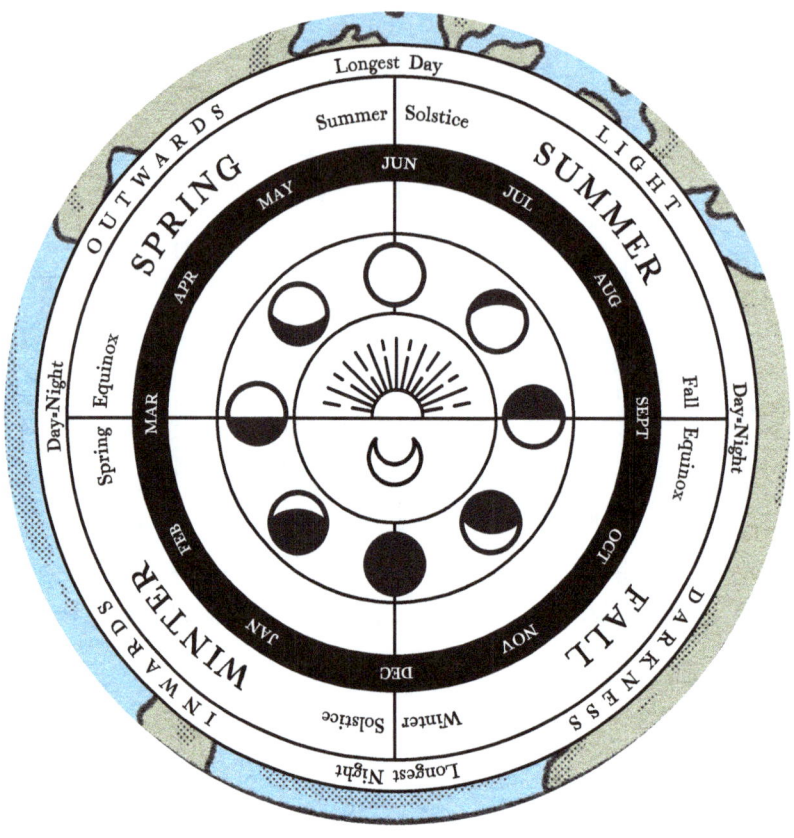

```
Draw a plant in its growth stages.
From stem and roots, to leaves, to flower, to end point.
```

rebirth **growth** **harvest** **rest**
SPRING SUMMER FALL WINTER

```
Write seasonal considerations on calendar pages
```

Moon	Month	Meaning
Wolf Moon	JAN	Purify
Snow Moon	FEB	Cleanse
Worm Moon	MAR	Prepare
Pink Moon	APR	Plant intention
Flower Moon	MAY	Nurture
Strawberry Moon	JUN	Absorb; start to reach outwards
Buck Moon	JUL	Grow; focus outwards
Sturgeon Moon	AUG	Harvest
Harvest Moon	SEPT	Gather
Hunters Moon	OCT	Transition; start to focus inwards
Beaver Moon	NOV	Death; reflect inwards
Cold Moon	DEC	Celebration; rebirth

MONTH

_____

SEASONAL CONSIDERATIONS

....
....
....
....
....
....
....
....
....
....

VIBE CHECK

MONDAY	TUESDAY	WEDNESDAY

PLANT · GROW · HARVEST · REST · REPEAT

Connect the dots

| THURSDAY | FRIDAY | SATURDAY | SUNDAY |

HABITS & DAILY PRACTICES

M T W T F S S
○○○○○○○
○○○○○○○
○○○○○○○
○○○○○○○
○○○○○○○

M T W T F S S
○○○○○○○
○○○○○○○
○○○○○○○
○○○○○○○
○○○○○○○

M T W T F S S
○○○○○○○
○○○○○○○
○○○○○○○
○○○○○○○
○○○○○○○

M T W T F S S
○○○○○○○
○○○○○○○
○○○○○○○
○○○○○○○
○○○○○○○

M T W T F S S
○○○○○○○
○○○○○○○
○○○○○○○
○○○○○○○
○○○○○○○

"We do not learn from experience... we learn from reflecting on experience." - John Dewey

MONTHLY BUDGET

_____

Add these totals together
for the expenses total

EXPENSES

Categories					
Total					

Expenses Total _____

INCOME

Source	Amount
Total	

REFUNDS

Source	Amount
Total	

TOP LINE BUDGET

Income _____
Refunds + _____
Incoming _____
Savings _____
Expenses + _____
Outgoing _____
Net Total _____

Add these totals to the quarterly budget page to find patterns and identify waste

```
  Incoming
- Outgoing
  Net Total
```

NOTES

"If you fail to plan, you are planning to fail!" - Benjamin Franklin

QUARTERLY BUDGET   MONTH 1   MONTH 2   MONTH 3

	MONTH 1	MONTH 2	MONTH 3
Income Totals			
Refund Totals +			
Incoming			
Savings Totals			
Expenses Totals +			
Outgoing			
Net Totals			

```
Net total is
what you have left.
1) Pay off debt
2) Save
3) Invest
```

REFLECTIONS

Any outstanding payments? Is there anywhere you can cut back? What are you saving for?

What relationships are you prioritizing?

Think about the people or things that feed your soul.
Acknowledge your gratitude for them.

Make lists here or reach out and share.

THE MOON

A meaningful beacon of hope, the moon holds great power in its consistency. Aligning yourself with the moon and its energy acknowledges nature's cyclical patterns and their impact on our body and spirit.

New Moon	First Quarter	Full Moon	Last Quarter	New Moon
Waxing Crescent	Waxing Gibbous	Waning Gibbous	Waning Crescent	

NEW MOON
Related to the dark moon, the new moon is a time for inspiration, dreaming, and brainstorming.

Characteristics: renewal, unlimited possibilities, inspiration

FIRST QUARTER
Build momentum and do the work. Ideas expand and take up more space and energy.

Characteristics: determination, focus, dedication

FULL MOON
A shining culmination of efforts, the full moon represents completion. Under the brightened sky, it's an ideal time for gathering to celebrate or for ritual practice.

Characteristics: celebration, rewards, power

LAST QUARTER
Prioritize reflection. Time to consider your efforts, adjust, and grow. Relinquish what's no longer needed and recognize what served you well.

Characteristics: organize, consider, optimize

MOON SCIENCE

Naturally a combination of dark gray and light green, the moon appears to glow, reflecting the light of the sun.

A celestial satellite, the moon makes a complete orbit around the earth every 27.3 days.

The moon is responsible for the gravitational effects of water in and on earth.

Human bodies are roughly 60-percent water. This accounts for the moon's pull on our bodies and spirit.

CONNECTING WITH THE MOON

Aligning with the moon helps us tap into our deeper selves to better understand our patterns.

Ways to Connect

RITUAL BATHS engage the senses and allow for focused exploration. Different phases support different characteristics.
TAROT aids in exploring inner self. Align with different moon phases to focus certain intentions.
PASSIVE THOUGHT OR MEDITATION connects you with how you're feeling during different phases.
DEDICATED SPACE for objects and materials honors the moon physically.

Materials

ORBS pay homage to the sun and the moon.
SHELLS represent the moon's power.
WATER is the moon's element.
MIRRORS mimic the moon's properties.

Write observations about your energy during different moon cycles under seasonal considerations on calendar pages.

I release the things
that no longer serve me

These cards are for you. You can burn them, soak them, keep them, or bury them.

These cards are for you. You can burn them, soak them, keep them, or bury them.

ACKNOWLEDGEMENTS

Karen O'Brien, my mother, I share every accomplishment with you. Thank you for always being my example.

Tim Drobniak, my love and best friend. Thank you for your support throughout this *sometimes* stressful process. You are the moon of my life.

You're a truly magical human, Didier Garcia. Your energy, skills, and expertise made this project possible and I'm endlessly grateful.

Natalia Navarra, your art is magnificent and breathes such life into these pages. Thank you for sharing.

Metaxia Papademetriou thank you for your witchy sisterhood and therapist know-how.

Hey Dutch Godshalk, thanks a million for your editing skills and for making sure I didn't use the wrong "their".

The individuals quoted within this guide have brought so much inspiration into the world. Let their contribution be recognized and appreciated.

Mother Nature, you're the queen of the universe. Thank you for sharing your magic so we can continue to learn and draw inspiration from it. I'll work to protect that magic for the rest of my life.

To the moon, I'm in awe of you. Let's keep flowing in the cycles of life.

To anyone who reads, uses, or enjoys this guide, thank you. I hope you get as much peace out of using it as I did creating it.

Moon

You're always the end,
and kind of the beginning.
You remind us of our past,
and what we want to start winning.

You bring intentions of change,
and salutations of growth.
You're a guiding marker,
an ancient beacon of hope.

I'm grateful to know that no matter the strife,
you'll always keep flowing with the cycles of life.